VOLUME

Chris Woodford

Gareth Stevens
Publishing

WHAT IS VOLUME?

One of the world's biggest airplanes is called the Airbus Beluga. It is named for a whale called the beluga. This airplane is so huge that it has enough space inside to carry about 50,000 basketballs. Another large airplane, the Boeing 747 Jumbo Jet, can carry 30,000 basketballs. A sport utility vehicle is much smaller. It can probably carry only 50 to 100 basketballs.

▼ **The world's largest cruise ship is called *Oasis of the Seas*. It has enough volume to carry about 80,000,000 basketballs.**

OASIS OF THE SEAS

The amount of space something can hold is called its volume. An Airbus Beluga has more volume than a Jumbo Jet because it can hold more things. A sport utility vehicle has less volume than a Jumbo Jet because it can hold fewer things.

We can also think of volume another way. Volume is the amount of space something takes up. Fifty thousand basketballs take up a certain volume— the same as the volume inside an Airbus Beluga.

▶ MEASURING AND COMPARING

We can measure a large volume by finding out how many times a smaller volume fits inside it. We do this when we say that an airplane holds 50,000 basketballs. We are measuring the airplane's volume by comparing it with the volume of a basketball.

1 basketball
x 50,000
= 1 Airbus
Beluga
airplane

WORD BANK   *Compare: look at two things to see if they are the same*

THREE DIMENSIONS

►►► **A** longer airplane usually has more volume than a shorter one. Length is not the only thing that changes volume, though. Suppose we could make the airplane wider or higher but keep it the same length. That would also increase the volume.

Just as volume is linked to length, it is also linked to area. Area is the size of a flat surface. If we made the size of an airplane's floor twice as big, but kept its height the same, then that would double the airplane's volume. And if we kept the airplane's floor the same but doubled its height, that would also double its volume.

◄ **When a balloon is blown up, its length may not increase very much, but its volume will increase by a lot.**

LENGTH, AREA, AND VOLUME

Length is a measurement in one direction. Sometimes we call this direction a dimension. To measure an area, we usually have to measure both its length and width. So area is a measurement in two directions, or dimensions. To find a thing's volume, we have to measure it in three directions. So, volume is a measurement in three dimensions: length, height, and width.

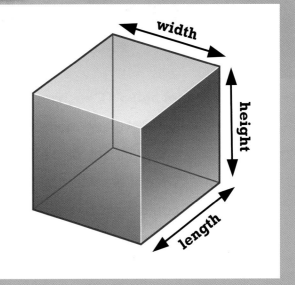

length x height x width = volume

Changing volumes

Length, area, and volume are linked. Making one of these things bigger usually makes all the others bigger, too.

However, this is not always true. For example, we could make an airplane just a little bit longer but only half as high and half as wide. Even though it was longer, that airplane would have less volume inside.

FACT

The biggest party balloons have a volume of 270 cubic feet.

VOLUMES OF LIQUIDS

People need to measure volume when they buy a liquid, such as gasoline. When they fill up their car's gas tank, they buy a certain number of gallons of gas. An airplane also has a fuel tank that holds a certain number of gallons of aviation fuel.

Measuring in gallons

A gallon is a measurement of a liquid's volume. It comes from the old word *galleta*, which meant "bucket." In olden times, when you bought a gallon of something, you were really buying a bucketful. A gallon is about the same volume as 230 cubic inches.

▶ This jug has a volume of 1 gallon, or 8 pints. Four quarts also make 1 gallon.

▶ THE TEN-GALLON HAT

Texans are known for their large ten-gallon hats. But if you filled a ten-gallon hat with water, it would hold only a few pints, not 10 gallons. Ten-gallon hats get their name from *galón*, the Spanish word for "braid," or ribbon. Ten-gallon hats were expensive hats decorated with ten colored braids or ribbons.

▶ A ten-gallon hat will not hold 10 gallons of water!

FACT

Some trucks have tanks that carry 200 gallons of fuel. Airplane fuel tanks are even bigger.

Quarts and pints

A quart is a smaller volume than a gallon. It takes 4 quarts to make a gallon. There are 2 pints in a quart, so there are 8 pints in a gallon.

When people cook, they use a much smaller unit of volume called a fluid ounce. There are 16 fluid ounces in a pint. Can you work out how many fluid ounces there are in a quart? How many fluid ounces are there in a gallon? (Answers on page 31.)

WORD BANK *Gallon: a measurement of volume equal to eight pints*

SPHERES AND CONES

▶▶▶ It is more difficult to find the volume of a curved object than a straight one. To work with curved objects, we have to use a special number called pi, which can also be written π. Pi always means the number 3.14. Sums called formulas use pi to figure out the volumes of curved shapes.

▼ The bigger the cylinders in a car's engine, the more power it can make. A car with a 2-liter engine has cylinders with a volume of 2 liters. That is twice as powerful as a car with a 1-liter engine.

Volumes of spheres

You can use a formula to figure out the volume of a sphere if you know its radius. (The radius is the distance from the sphere's center to the outside.) That formula is:

**volume of sphere =
1.33 x pi x radius x radius x radius**

The radius of this sphere is 1 inch. So, its volume is:

1.33 x pi x 1 x 1 x 1
= about 4 cubic inches (4 in^3)
(4.18 in^3 more accurately)

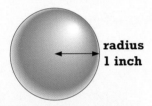

radius
1 inch

Volumes of cones

There are also formulas for figuring out the volume of more complicated shapes, such as cones and cylinders:

**volume of cone =
0.33 x pi x radius x radius x height of cone**

**volume of cylinder =
pi x radius x radius x height of cylinder**

The radius of this cone is 1 inch. The cone is 2.5 inches tall. So, its volume is:

0.33 x pi x 1 x 1 x 2.5
= 2.5 cubic inches (2.5 in^3)
(2.59 in^3 more accurately)

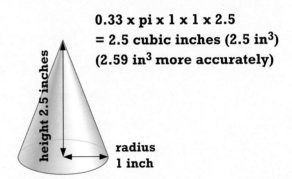

height 2.5 inches

radius
1 inch

▶ TRY THIS

+ – = x + – = x + – = x + – = x + – = x + –

MEASURE THIS CYLINDER

Can you figure out the volume of this cylinder? Remember:

pi x radius x radius x height = volume

Answer on page 31.

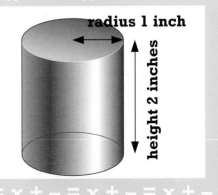

radius 1 inch

height 2 inches

+ – = x + – = x + – = x + – = x + – = x + – = x + –

TOUGHER VOLUMES

▶▶▶ **S**ome objects have tricky shapes. So how do we find their volume? Many everyday objects are made up of simpler ones. For example, a dome is half of a sphere. Its volume is equal to the volume of a sphere divided by two. In another example, a pencil is a bit like a cone stuck to a cylinder.

Adding the parts together

We can always calculate the volume of an object by trying to find simpler objects inside it. We can figure out the volume of each of these simple objects. Then we can add together their volumes to find the volume of the whole object. So the volume of the whole object is the volume of the parts added together.

pyramid with square base

cube

◀▶ **These more complicated objects can be broken down into a cube plus a square pyramid (left) and a cylinder plus a cone (right). Then it is easy to figure out the volume of each object.**

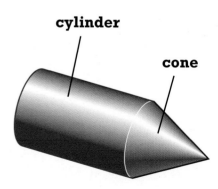

cylinder

cone

HOW BIG IS THE CAPITOL?

Suppose you wanted to find out the volume of the U.S. Capitol in Washington, D.C. If you look closely, you can see that the building is made up of a dome, sitting on a cylinder, which sits on several boxes. A dome is a sphere cut in half. So the volume of the Capitol is half the volume of a sphere, plus the volume of the cylinder, plus the volume of the boxes beneath the cylinder.

FACT

A junior basketball has a volume of about 380 cubic inches (that is 6,227 cubic centimeters).

▼ The cylinder under the dome of the Capitol is called the Rotunda. Its volume is 1.3 million cubic feet.

ESTIMATES AND GUESSES

We cannot always measure things exactly. We cannot easily measure the volume of our planet, Earth. But we can still guess its volume. Suppose we could find a box big enough to hold Earth. If we could measure the volume of the box, that would tell us roughly how big Earth is. But Earth would fit inside the box with room to spare. So our measurement of volume is only really a good guess. We call a measurement like that an estimate.

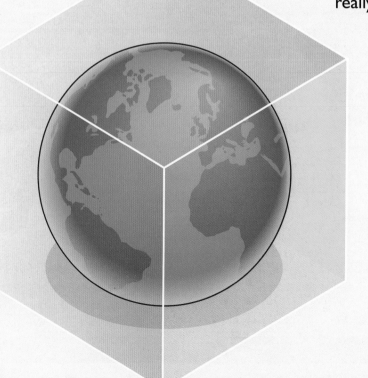

◀ If we could fit Earth inside a huge box, then the volume of the box would give us an estimate of the volume of Earth. The box would be larger than Earth, of course.

Making an estimate

An estimate is sometimes the best measurement we can make. An example of an estimate is explaining the volume of an airplane by saying how many basketballs would fit inside it. The basketballs do not fill up the plane completely. There are spaces between the balls. So when we say a Jumbo Jet holds 30,000 basketballs, that is an estimate of the airplane's volume. It is not an exact measurement.

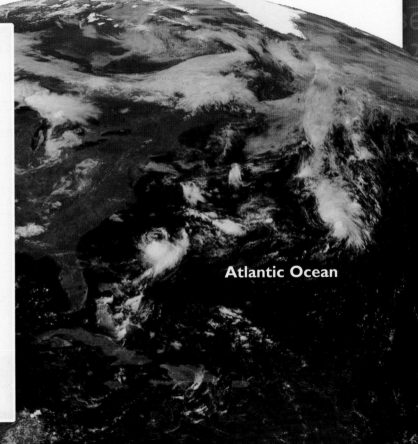

▶ HOW MUCH WATER?

The Atlantic Ocean covers an area of about 41 million square miles (106 million square kilometers). On average, it is 2 miles (3.5 kilometers) deep. We can estimate the volume of the Atlantic by multiplying these two numbers. That gives a volume of 85 million cubic miles (355 million cubic kilometers). That is only an estimate because the ocean is not the same depth all over.

Atlantic Ocean

WORD BANK   *Estimate: a rough measurement; a good guess*

LIQUIDS, SOLIDS, AND GASES

W ater is an amazing substance. Without water, no animals or plants could live on Earth. Like many other substances, water can take different forms—solid ice, liquid water, and a gas called steam.

The same amount of water takes up different volumes when it is ice, water, or steam. Unlike other liquids, when water freezes into ice, it takes up more volume. When the ice warms up, it melts into cold water. That takes up less room. But hot water takes up more volume than cold water. Steam spreads out to take up the most volume of all.

▶ The water in this bottle froze to become ice. But ice takes up more volume than water. The glass bottle could not contain the ice, and the glass shattered.

▶ AMAZING AEROGEL

Aerogels are chemicals that were invented in the 1930s. They are solids, but most of the volume they take up is air, so they weigh almost nothing. They have lots of different uses. One is to make very warm and very light clothes. Another is to make windows that trap the heat.

Making steam

When you watch an adult boil a kettle, you can see that a small amount of water can turn into huge clouds of steam. If we cool down steam, we can change it back into liquid water. That makes it take up a smaller volume. We can also make the volume of steam smaller by squeezing it. That is called putting water under pressure. We can do that by pushing together the steam particles in a special container.

▶ Everything is made up of tiny invisible particles called atoms. Atoms join to form molecules. The molecules in a solid are packed closely together. The molecules in a liquid spread out to the shape of the container. The molecules in a gas spread out as far as they can. So a gas takes up the most volume.

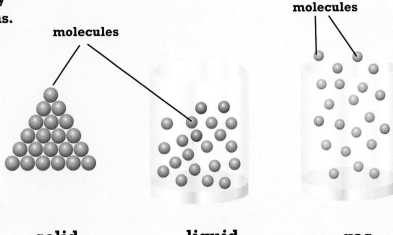

molecules

molecules

solid   **liquid**   **gas**

WORD BANK   *Freeze: when water gets so cold it turns to a solid*

HOW VOLUMES CHANGE

We might think that volumes always stay the same, but that is not true. If you put a glass of cold water in sunshine, heat makes the water molecules move around more. Each molecule takes up more space. So hot water takes up more volume than cold water because it expands, or grows larger.

▼ **Great firework displays like this are caused by chemical reactions. The reactions create chemicals with larger volumes.**

▶ HOW EXPLOSIONS WORK

Substances such as gunpowder and dynamite are explosives—they cause explosions. When heated, explosives change from solids to gases. They expand very quickly and make a huge volume of gas. To start with, explosives take up very little volume. But the gas they make takes up much more volume. As the gas is produced, it can make a violent explosion, which can blow out windows or even knock down whole buildings.

FACT

The most powerful fireworks can shoot 1,300 feet (400 meters) into the sky.

More heat, more volume

You can sometimes see power lines stretching lower in the summer than in the winter. Again, heat makes the metal wires expand and take up more volume. Even a huge building like the U.S. Capitol expands slightly in hot weather. So it takes up very slightly more volume in summer than in winter!

The volumes of things can also change during a chemical reaction. That is what happens when we mix chemicals together. We make new chemicals that take up more volume than the ones we started with. It is chemical reactions—and the changes in volume that they cause—that make fireworks explode.

WORD BANK *Reaction: something that happens when chemicals mix*

HUGE VOLUMES

Everything around Earth, including the stars and space, is called the universe. No one knows how big the universe is. It is constantly expanding. Its volume is always getting bigger. Volumes on Earth are much smaller, but they can still be pretty amazing.

Water, water, water

Every day, on average, every person in the United States uses 69 gallons (314 liters) of water. That

▼ A big chunk of ice falls into the sea in Antarctica. If Earth gets warmer, more ice will melt, and the volume of the oceans will get bigger.

▶ HUGE BUILDING

The Aerium, in Germany, is one of the world's biggest buildings. It was built to house a huge airship, but it is now a vacation resort. The Aerium has a volume of 194 million cubic feet (5.5 million cubic meters). That's big enough to hold the water from 2,200 Olympic-size swimming pools! The Aerium's swimming pool has room for 8,000 people.

▲ The volume of the Aerium is enormous—big enough to fit 200 million basketballs.

includes water for washing, drinking, cleaning cars, and making things in factories. It is still only a tiny amount of our planet's total volume of water. Earth contains a truly astonishing 330 million cubic miles (about 1,300 million cubic kilometers) of water!

Much of Earth's water is frozen as ice near the North and South Poles. If all that ice melted, the volume of the oceans would increase enormously. The sea level might rise up to 200 feet (60 meters) over the whole Earth. Many of our towns and cities would then be flooded!

FACT

The volume of the Empire State Building is 37 million cubic feet (1 million cubic meters).

WORD BANK   *Expanding: the way that something is getting bigger*

HANDS ON

CHANGING SHAPES, SAME VOLUMES

YOU WILL NEED

- Some modeling clay
- Two rulers
- A pen and piece of paper

WHAT TO DO

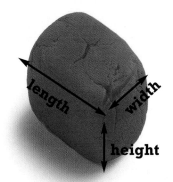

2. Squeeze the ball between the two rulers to make all the sides flat.

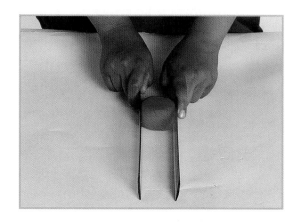

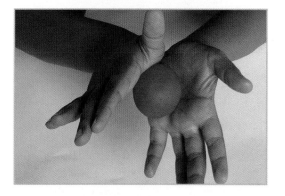

I. You need to make the modeling clay into a cube. A cube is as tall as it is wide and long. So, it is easier to make a cube if you first roll the clay into a ball. Make sure the ball is not oval (like a small football).

3. Measure the length, width, and height of your cube. These measurements should all be the same on a cube. Keep molding and measuring the clay until you have an exact cube.

4. When you have an exact cube, measure the length, width, and height in inches. Write these measurements down. Then use this sum to figure out your cube's volume:

length x width x height = volume

Because you measured the cube in inches, the volume is in cubic inches. Write "cubic inches" after the answer.

This may help ...

Sometimes the modeling clay may stick to the rulers and pull your cube apart. Try spraying a little cooking oil on the rulers before you start to squeeze the clay. This usually helps.

5. Make your cube into a longer box shape. Squeeze it between the two rulers to make the sides flat. Do not add or take away any clay.

length

6. Repeat step 4 to calculate the volume of your new shape.

7. Compare the volumes of your two shapes. The two measurements should be the same. The cube and the box are different shapes, but they have the same volume.

GLOSSARY

area The amount of space that a surface takes up.

comparing A way of looking at two things together to see if they are the same or different.

cube A box-shaped object.

cubic foot A volume measuring one foot long by one foot high by one foot wide.

cubic inch A volume measuring one inch in each direction.

cubic meter A volume measuring one meter in each direction.

cubic mile A volume measuring one mile in each direction.

cubic unit A unit for measuring volumes.

dimension A direction in which we measure something. Lengths are measured in one dimension, areas in two dimensions, and volumes in three dimensions.

distance The length between two points.

estimate A rough measurement; sometimes just a good guess.

expand The way in which something gets bigger.

fluid ounce A small measurement of liquid volume.

formula A type of math we can use to work out a measurement.

gallon A measurement of volume. A gallon is equal to four quarts.

imperial Customary way of measuring things, which includes pints, quarts, and gallons.

liter A metric measurement of volume equal to a quarter of a gallon.

metric A way of measuring things based on the number 10. A liter is a metric measurement.

pi A special number used to work

out areas and volumes with curves. Pi has the value 3.14 and is often written with the Greek symbol π.

pint A measurement of volume. A large glass holds a pint of liquid.

quart A measurement of volume. There are two pints in a quart.

reaction In chemistry, something that happens when two different substances are added together.

unit A measurement of something. Examples of volume units are cubic inches, pints, gallons, and liters.

FIND OUT MORE

BOOKS

Thomas Adamson, *How Do You Measure Liquids?* Mankato, MN: Capstone, 2011.

Jennifer Roy, *Measuring at Home*. New York: Marshall Cavendish Benchmark, 2007.

Brian Sargent, *How Much Does It Hold?* New York: Children's Press, 2006.

Navin Sullivan, *Area, Distance, and Volume*. New York: Marshall Cavendish Benchmark, 2007.

Lisa Trumbauer, *What Is Volume?* New York: Children's Press, 2006.

WEBSITES

Johnnie's Math Page
Measurement puzzles designed to increase your ability to measure.
http://jmathpage.com/JIMSMeasurementlengthmass volume.html

Volume conversion chart
Convert volumes from imperial to metric and from metric to imperial.
http://www.sciencemadesimple.com/volume_conversion.php

Publisher's note to educators and parents: Our editors have carefully reviewed these websites to ensure that they are suitable for students. Many websites change frequently, however, and we cannot guarantee that a site's future contents will continue to meet our high standards of quality and educational value. Be advised that students should be closely supervised whenever they access the Internet.

Answers to questions
Page 8: The volume of the cube is 729 cubic inches; the basketball has a smaller volume
Page 11: There are 32 fluid ounces in 1 quart and 128 fluid ounces in 1 gallon
Page 13: 1 cubic meter = 35 cubic feet; 1 pint = about ½ liter; 1 quart = about 1 liter; 1 gallon = about 4 liters; 1 liter = 1¾ pints; 1 liter = about ¼ gallon
Page 17: The volume of the cylinder is 6.28 cubic inches

INDEX